THE WORLD OF
**VIDEO
GAMES**

YOUTH
AND VIDEO GAMES

By Ashley Strehle Hartman

ReferencePoint
Press®

San Diego, CA

© 2019 ReferencePoint Press, Inc.
Printed in the United States

For more information, contact:
ReferencePoint Press, Inc.
PO Box 27779
San Diego, CA 92198
www.ReferencePointPress.com

LIBRARY OF CONGRESS CATALOGING-IN-PUBLICATION DATA

Name: Strehle Hartman, Ashley, 1986– author.
Title: Youth and Video Games/by Ashley Strehle Hartman.
Description: San Diego, CA: ReferencePoint Press, Inc., [2019] | Series: The World of Video
Games | Audience: Grade 9 to 12 | Includes bibliographical references and index.
ISBN: 978-1-68282-565-5 (hardback)
ISBN: 978-1-68282-566-2 (ebook)
The complete Library of Congress record is available at www.loc.gov.

CONTENTS

IMPORTANT EVENTS IN THE HISTORY OF
VIDEO GAMES

1993
Senator Joseph Lieberman holds the first federal hearings on violent video games and their effects on children.

1999
After the Columbine High Scho shooting, victims' families sue video game developers. They claim that violent video games led the shooters to violence.

1978
Space Invaders is released. Its popularity with youth inspires controversy.

1960	1970	1980	1990	1995

1972
Atari releases *Pong*, a black-and-white video game with a bouncing ball. It becomes a major hit with youth and adults.

1994
The video game industry creates the Entertainment Software Ratings Board to assign ratings to video games.

1989
Nintendo introduces players to handheld video gaming with the Game Boy video game device.

1997
The first video game in the popular and controversial Grand Theft Auto series is released by Rockstar Games.

2002
US representative Joe Baca introduces the Protect Children from Video Game Sex and Violence Act of 2002, which would have made it illegal to sell M-rated games to minors.

2010
The Kaiser Family Foundation finds that youth between the ages of 8 and 18 spend an average of seven and half hours each day using electronic screens.

2017
The video game company Epic releases the video game *Fortnite*, which instantly becomes popular with youth around the world.

2016
Pokémon Go is released and thousands of youth around the world play the game on their mobile devices.

2000　　**2005**　　**2010**　　**2015**　　**2020**

2006
Nintendo releases the Nintendo Wii, which features wireless remotes and built-in Wi-Fi. It has many nonviolent, multiplayer games that appeal to a wide variety of gamers.

2018
President Donald Trump holds a meeting to discuss violent video games and their effect on youth.

2011
In a 7-2 decision, the Supreme Court strikes down a California state law that had attempted to ban the sale of violent video games to minors.

2012
The mobile game *Angry Birds* makes $200 million in this year alone.

REACHING YOUTH

Eleven-year-old Jordan puzzled over what obstacle to add to his maze. He already had a waterfall, some crushing walls, and several other traps for players to find. Jordan wanted his friends to face something unpredictable. Then he had an idea. He placed a cow in a pen and put pressure-sensitive plates on the ground. When the cow stepped on the plates, something unpredictable happened in the maze. Jordan smiled. He had figured out his maze. But this maze wasn't in his backyard or even drawn on a piece of paper. It was created in the video game *Minecraft*.

Minecraft is all about blocks. Released in 2009, the game is incredibly popular, with over 75 million monthly players in 2017. Within the game's virtual world, players mine and harvest cubes that they can use to build things. They can craft swords, circuits, and even cakes in single-player mode or online with users from around the world. According to Jordan, "It's like the earth, the world, and you're the creator of it."[1]

EDUCATIONAL VIDEO GAMES

Minecraft has a follow-up educational version, *MinecraftEdu*. In *MinecraftEdu*, teachers can control the game's world to create specific projects and lessons. As of 2016, *Minecraft* was being used as a teaching tool in more than 7,000 classrooms. *Minecraft* and

Players can build things in Minecraft *using items shaped like cubes. They can store items in chests for later use.*

MinecraftEdu have been used to teach art, math, science, and creative writing. Anthony Salcito of Microsoft, the company that owns *Minecraft*, states that "By creating a virtual world [in *Minecraft*] and then advancing in it, students can learn digital citizenship, empathy, social skills and even improve their literacy—while getting real time feedback on their problem-solving skills from the teacher."[2]

This isn't the first time video games have been used in the classroom. Teachers have been using video games since 1979 when the video game *The Oregon Trail* was introduced. It taught students about westward expansion in the United States. The multiple games in the Oregon Trail series simulate the experience of traveling the

7

Oregon Trail during the 1800s. Players face the same challenges as early settlers, such as harsh winters, starvation, and diseases.

A 2014 survey found that 55 percent of teachers use video games in the classroom, and all of these teachers use video games at least once per week. Studies show that video games keep students more engaged. They also affect how youth think. William Winn is the head of the Learning Center at the University of Washington's Human Interface Technology Laboratory. He believes that people who grew up playing video games think differently than other people. "They leap around. It's as though their cognitive structures were parallel, not sequential," he said.[3] As far back as the 1980s, researchers found that youth who played video games had improved skills in areas such as hand-eye coordination. Additional research has also found that video games improve visual memory in children.

> **"They leap around. It's as though their cognitive structures were parallel, not sequential."[3]**
>
> *–William Winn, head of the Learning Center at the University of Washington's Human Interface Technology Laboratory*

Many people support the use of video games in education. However, some people think video games are not the best way to reach youth. For example, pediatrician Dr. Scott Krugman is concerned that "many programs students use in school are entertainment and gamified."[4] When something is gamified, it means that game-like qualities have been added to it to make it more fun, or to encourage people to use it. In her book *Reset Your Child's Brain,* Dr. Victoria Dunckley voiced her concerns about gamified learning tools. She wrote, "The excitement about using electronic media to engage students has led to a rush to implement electronic learning tools, despite their poor track record in studies. . . . Soon enough, the novelty wears off, and more and more stimulation is required for focus."[5]

Despite these concerns, some people argue that video games are a part of life now. They see video games as a healthy part of the youth experience. In his book *Don't Bother Me Mom—I'm Learning*, author Marc Prensky wrote, "Part of our responsibility as adults is to make sure our children lead healthy, balanced lives. . . . [Video] games can—and should be—a vital part of that balance."[6]

Whether or not they are used in classrooms, youth are learning by playing video games. By having the cow walk over pressure plates, Jordan added a random element to his *Minecraft* maze. Other *Minecraft* players learn programming languages to give themselves stronger weapons, make their characters run faster, or eliminate enemies in the game. Jordan posted a sign at the end of his maze that read, "The journey matters more than what you get in the end."[7] The relationship between youth and video games has been a controversial topic for several decades, with experts on both sides disagreeing on how much time children should interact with video games. Still, with video games becoming more accessible at home and in schools, youth will continue interacting with video game technology in their daily lives.

CHAPTER 1

HOW DO YOUTH USE
VIDEO GAMES?

Youth have access to a variety of video games. They range from quick, casual games to complex strategy-based games. The video game industry defines casual games as video games people can learn easily and play quickly. These simple games, such as *Tetris* and *Angry Birds*, are usually played online or on smartphones. They do not require a lot of computer memory or processing power. People who play these games may do so for only a few minutes a day, a couple of times a week.

Complex games require more commitment. They can take as many as one hundred or more hours to complete. These games, such as *The Legend of Zelda: Breath of the Wild* and *Dragon Age: Inquisition*, are harder to learn and full of complicated tasks. Players have to learn new skills and strategies. Within the game, they may have to make difficult decisions that will affect relationships and storylines. Massively multiplayer online games (MMOs) are popular complex games. These games, such as *World of Warcraft*, allow millions of people across the globe to connect in fantasy worlds. People explore these games using their characters, often known as avatars, while they participate in quests or raids.

World of Warcraft *is a popular video game for youth and adults. People gather to play it at conventions and trade shows.*

Players tend to invest a lot of time into MMOs because these games are designed to be played for long periods. In his book *Game Frame: Using Games as a Strategy for Success*, Aaron Dignan wrote that MMOs can also encourage video game players to think critically, as these games often require players to use "long-term nested problem solving."[8] These are situations in which players have an overall goal that's impossible to achieve until the player has solved other problems. "For example, if you want to save the princess, first you must cross the river. To do that, you need to build a boat. To do that, you need lumber. To get that, you need an ax, and so on," Dignan explained.[9]

MMOs and other complex games can provide opportunities for learning, but they are not specifically designed to be educational.

> ❝Today, serious games are everywhere . . . [and] new applications are cropping up every day.❞[11]
>
> *–Aaron Dignan, author of Game Frame: Using Games as a Strategy for Success*

MinecraftEdu and earlier games like *Oregon Trail* are examples of games that were created to teach. According to Dignan, these "serious games" are "designed for a purpose beyond entertainment."[10] They were developed after academic institutions and companies noticed that video games could be used as learning tools. Serious games are usually designed for a specific, practical use. For example, in addition to teaching children, serious games may be used by companies or other groups for job training. Serious games are becoming increasingly popular. "Today, serious games are everywhere . . . [and] new applications are cropping up every day," Dignan wrote.[11]

PERSONALIZING THE VIDEO GAME EXPERIENCE

Because of the variety of video games, players can choose exactly the type of gaming experience they want. As video game developer Jane McGonigal wrote in *Reality Is Broken: Why Games Make Us Better and How They Can Change the World*, gamers can "choose from among five-second minigames, ten-minute casual games, eight-hour action games, and role-playing games that go on endlessly twenty-four hours a day, three hundred sixty-five days

Some video games require people to get up and move around. They may have players jump, dance, or swing a controller like a tennis racket.

a year."[12] Players can also choose games with scores or without scores, and they can play games with or without stories. McGonigal suggests that video games also provide players with different kinds of challenges, or work, they find rewarding.

Action games such as the racing game *Gran Turismo* or the zombie game *Left 4 Dead* give players high-stakes work. These games are fast-paced and they get players' hearts pumping because they are so dramatic. "It's the risk of crashing, burning or having our brains sucked out that makes us feel more alive," McGonigal wrote.[13] Games can also provide people with busywork. This repetitive work could be monotonous if it wasn't fun. In the causal game,

Bejeweled, for example, players have to organize multicolored jewels into certain patterns. This keeps players' hands and minds busy and leaves them feeling accomplished.

Some video games provide more complicated challenges called mental work. In Nintendo's *Brain Age* games, for example, players have to quickly answer math problems. McGonigal said these games make players feel accomplished because they feel like they are improving their minds. Others such as *Wii Boxing* or *Dance Dance Revolution* provide players with real physical work. These games give players a workout by raising their heart rates and making them sweat. With the variety of video games available today, players can find games that challenge both their brains and their bodies.

This variety of video games means there is something for everyone, and it seems like almost every youth is playing video games. According to a survey from the Entertainment Software Association (ESA), a trade organization for the video game industry, "97 percent of youth play computer and video games."[14] In a survey released in 2017, the ESA also found that youth make up a sizable portion of the overall gaming population. Though the average gamer is thirty-five years old, males under the age of eighteen make up 18 percent of gamers and females under the age of eighteen make up 11 percent of gamers.

YOUTH AND THE RISE OF VIDEO GAMES

Today's youth are able to play many different video games on their phones, computers, or dedicated gaming consoles. But youth didn't always have these options. Though the first video game was created in 1958, video game play didn't really hit it off with youth until decades later. It wasn't until the late 1970s and early 1980s that video games became very popular with children and teens. They could play games

VIDEO GAME DEMOGRAPHICS

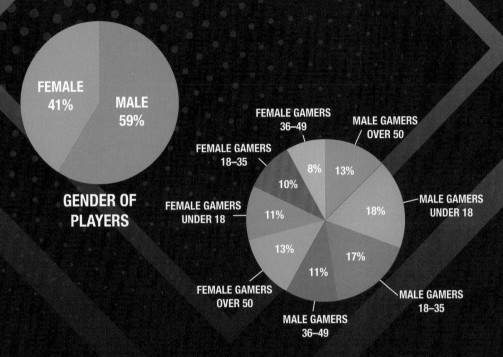

GENDER OF PLAYERS

FEMALE 41%

MALE 59%

FEMALE GAMERS 36–49 — 8%

MALE GAMERS OVER 50 — 13%

FEMALE GAMERS 18–35 — 10%

MALE GAMERS UNDER 18 — 18%

FEMALE GAMERS UNDER 18 — 11%

MALE GAMERS 18–35 — 17%

FEMALE GAMERS OVER 50 — 13%

MALE GAMERS 36–49 — 11%

These charts show a breakdown of video game players by age and gender. As the graph shows, 18 percent of video game players are males less than eighteen years old. Eleven percent of video game players are females less than eighteen years old. The graph also shows that there are video game players of all ages. Though the majority of male gamers are under eighteen years old, the majority of female gamers are more than fifty years old. The numbers in the chart at right do not add to 100 percent due to rounding.

The data from this graph comes from the Entertainment Software Association (ESA), a trade organization for the video game industry. It was taken from the ESA's "2017 Sales, and Usage Data: Essential Facts about the Computer and Video Game Industry" report which studied the video game habits of Americans. This survey looked at the video game usage of 4,000 US households.

on home consoles such as the Atari 2600 or the Magnavox Odyssey, or head to arcades and play games there.

Video game arcades were a popular hangout for youth in the 1980s. The games featured there, such as *Pac-Man* and *Space Invaders,* were pop culture phenomena. In 1982, *Time* magazine featured a cover that read "GRONK! FLASH! ZAP! Video Games are Blitzing the World!"[15] That same year, the song "Pac-Man Fever" by the band Buckner and Garcia was a Top 40 hit on the radio. Also in 1982, the movie *Fast Times at Ridgemont High* had several scenes in which teens hung out in a video game arcade. Arcades weren't just making the news, they were also making a lot of money. According to Dignan, "as far back as 1981, arcades around the country were collecting 20 billion quarters a year. That's a $5 billion dollar gaming market that had to be made one coin at a time."[16]

But, as arcades became more popular, they also become more controversial. Medical professionals, media commentators, government officials, and teachers claimed video games would cause problems such as eye damage or a condition they called "Space Invaders Wrist." They were also concerned that video games would lead teenagers into harmful behaviors. As Michael Z. Newman wrote in an article for *Smithsonian.com*: "The arcades where many teenagers played video games were imagined as dens of vice. . . . Kids who went to play *Tempest* or *Donkey Kong* might end up seduced by lowlifes, spiraling into lives of substance abuse, sexual depravity and crime."[17]

News articles at the time claimed that video games led to more crime. Government officials in Japan became concerned after a twelve-year-old fan of the arcade game *Space Invaders* tried to rob a bank with a shotgun. He later admitted he wanted more coins to play the popular video game. In England, police blamed *Space Invaders* for the increased divorce rate.

In light of these news reports and the controversy surrounding video games, city governments attempted to regulate arcades. For example, the city of Mesquite, Texas, barred youth under the age of seventeen from a local arcade unless they were accompanied by a parent or guardian. The company that owned the arcade sued the city and the case made its way to the Supreme Court. Though the Supreme Court sent it back to the appeals court in 1982 without a ruling, it wouldn't be the last time government officials sought to regulate how youth interacted with video games.

> **"The arcades where many teenagers played video games were imagined as dens of vice. . . . Kids who went to play *Tempest* or *Donkey Kong* might end up seduced by lowlifes, spiraling into lives of substance abuse, sexual depravity and crime."** [17]
>
> *–Michael Z. Newman, writer for Smithsonian.com*

Even though video games and arcades had critics in the 1970s and 1980s, they had supporters too. According to Newman, some adults did not see video games as worthless entertainment, but instead as "essential tools for training young people for a future of high-tech, computerized work and leisure."[18] Some educators agreed too—which is what led to the introduction of video games in schools. The video game developer Minnesota Educational Computing Consortium (MECC) partnered with the then-unknown computer corporation Apple in 1985. Together, the two companies sold the video game *The Oregon Trail* to school districts across the country.

THE SPREAD OF *THE OREGON TRAIL*

In 1971 Don Rawitsch was teaching history at an elementary school. He drew the 2,000-mile Oregon Trail journey on a piece of paper. Rawitsch wrote in the obstacles pioneers would have faced along the way such as bad weather, illness, and lack of food. Then he showed the sketch to his roommates Paul Dillenberger and Bill Heinemann, who had experience with a coding language called BASIC. Dillenberger and Heinemann turned the sketch into a game that could be played on a teletype machine, which was like a computer without a screen. The teletype machine would print instructions for players to follow. It would also print out the consequences of their actions. For example, players could type "BANG" into the teletype machine to hunt. Then, the teletype machine would print out a paper telling them whether or not they had hit their target.

Three years later, Rawitsch typed up the code and submitted it to the Minnesota Educational Computing Consortium (MECC). Thanks to MECC, *The Oregon Trail* was released to students throughout Minnesota. When MECC made a deal with Apple, the game appeared in classrooms across the country. It was frequently played in schools in the 1980s and 1990s, and it's still available today on browsers. Players in *Minecraft* can even access *The Oregon Trail*'s virtual world.

The game and its sequels would be popular in the classroom for the next two decades, selling more than 65 million copies.

YOUTH AND A GROWING VIDEO GAME MARKET

In the late 1980s and early 1990s, video game companies created different types of video games and gaming platforms to compete with each other. This changed how youth could access video games. For example, Nintendo released the Game Boy in 1989. It was an 8-bit video game device, which means that the computer inside was able to process 8 bits of information at a time. The Game Boy allowed for handheld gaming. Children and teens no longer needed to play video games in arcades or on the gaming console in their parents' basement. They could now take their favorite video games such as *Tetris* and *The Legend of Zelda: Link's Awakening* with them to school, to their friends' houses, and on long car trips.

The Game Boy was just one of many video game systems that Nintendo released in the late 1980s and early 1990s. During this time period, Nintendo competed with fellow console developer Sega. According to the BBC's technology desk editor, Leo Kelion, the competition between these companies "laid the foundations of the video games industry as we know it today."[19] As the two companies fought to outdo their competitor, they both created popular video game franchises and characters such as Mario and Sonic the Hedgehog. They also both released versions of the street-fighting game *Mortal Kombat*.

Mortal Kombat would go on to have a major impact on the way video games were marketed and sold to youth. *Mortal Kombat* started out as an arcade game that was controversial for how it portrayed violence. It featured blood and gore and allowed players to rip out characters' spines and hearts. According to the author of *Jacked: The Outlaw Story of Grand Theft Auto*, David Kushner, "*Mortal Kombat* brought interactive violence of a kind never before seen in living rooms."[20] Though *Mortal Kombat* wasn't very realistic, writer Kat Eschner noted for *Smithsonian.com* that it "was staggeringly violent and extremely gory for its time. When parents saw their children decapitating opponents amidst splashes of blood and guts, reactions were . . . less than amazing."[21] When Nintendo converted the game into a version for its home console, programmers removed some of

Senator Joe Lieberman held the first federal hearing on violent video games in 1993. It led to the creation of the ESRB.

the violent elements and even re-colored the blood and gore green to make it less realistic. Taking the opposite approach, Sega increased the violence in its version of the game for its own home console. Even the toned-down version of the game that Nintendo released caused controversy, as it was a far cry from Nintendo's other available games. According to Eschner, Nintendo was known for releasing "relatively cute and cuddly Super Nintendo games like *Super Mario Bros.* and *Donkey Kong. Mortal Kombat* was not that type of game."[22]

The matter came to a head in the early 1990s, when Connecticut senator Joe Lieberman started a campaign against *Mortal Kombat* and other violent video games. The game led Lieberman to hold the first federal hearing on violent video games and their effects on children in December 1993. In response to these hearings, the US video game industry created the Entertainment Software Ratings Board (ESRB) to give ratings to their games. The ESRB would go on to give *Mortal Kombat* a "mature" rating, meaning it was only recommended for gamers 17 and older.

NEW WAYS TO PLAY

In the 2000s and 2010s, the rising popularity of smartphones gave youth the option to play video games through new platforms such as downloadable apps. Youth could now play video games anywhere with Wi-Fi or cell phone reception. A 2016 study by the nonprofit group Common Sense Media looked at the media habits of teens between the ages of thirteen and eighteen. They found that teens in this age group spent about eighty minutes per day playing video games on different platforms such as on consoles, computers, or mobile devices.

Pokémon Go, released in 2016, broke many video game records. By 2018, it had been downloaded more than 800 million times and generated more than $2 billion in revenue. The game was so popular in part because it gave many video game players their first experience with augmented reality (AR). AR allows for computer-generated information to be placed digitally in the player's real-life surroundings through a mobile camera. In the case of *Pokémon Go,* virtual creatures seem to appear in real-world locations such as parks and neighborhoods. Players battle the creatures to defeat opponents at Gyms. *Pokémon Go* needs to be played on the go. Pokémon do not appear on the screen unless the player moves around outside. As JV Chamary wrote for *Forbes.com,* "Anyone whose childhood included video games in front of the TV will have heard parents yell, 'Go play

> **"**Anyone whose childhood included video games in front of the TV will have heard parents yell, 'Go play outside!' Well, *Pokémon Go* forces you to do just that.**"**[23]
>
> –JV Chamary, writer

outside!' Well, *Pokémon Go* forces you to do just that."[23]

Though some people praise *Pokémon Go* because it encourages players to get outside and get exercise, others worry that the game may be dangerous. Since *Pokémon Go* requires players to walk around in the real world, parents worry that children will become so absorbed in the game, they will miss real world dangers such as oncoming traffic.

INCREASING INTERACTION WITH VIDEO GAMES

In 2017, the free, multiplayer game *Fortnite* was released. *Fortnite* is available on a variety of platforms such as gaming consoles, computers, and mobile devices. As of June 2018, more than 125 million people were playing *Fortnite*, from children to adults. As writer Katia Moskvitch states, "during the Football World Cup, goal scorers like England's Deli Alli and France's Antoine Griezmann celebrated [goals] with *Fortnite* emotes," or dances from the game.[24] Moskvitch's ten-year old son couldn't get enough of the game: "He watches *Fortnite* videos on YouTube. He is constantly emoting. It's been months—and *Fortnite* is all he and his friends talk about."[25]

Professionals are less worried about *Fortnite*'s effects on youth players. Professor Andy Przybylski, director of Research at the University of Oxford's Internet Institute, believes that *Fortnite* will continue to make the news until a new game becomes popular. He adds:

There will simply be another craze. And they'll interview another headteacher who banned it in her school, and they'll interview a parent, and they'll interview a clinician, and they'll all make all the same kind of statements about that game. . . . We'll have forgotten about how worried we were about World of Warcraft, *and how worried we were about* Pokémon Go . . . *and how worried we were about* Fortnite. . . . And Fortnite *will be forgotten.*[26]

> **"We'll have forgotten about how worried we were about *World of Warcraft*, and how worried we were about *Pokémon Go* . . . and how worried we were about *Fortnite*. . . . And *Fortnite* will be forgotten."**[26]
>
> –Andy Przybylski, director of Research at the University of Oxford's Internet Institute

This cycle of hit games and parental concern may become more common in years to come as video games become an even more ingrained part of youth's lives. As Dignan wrote, "Seeing games as somehow distinct from everyday life is going to get harder and harder. Games are everywhere, and they're blurring the lines between play and reality."[27]

HOW DO VIDEO GAMES
AFFECT YOUTH?

Video games are a common part of youth's lives. Though many people worry that this is harmful for youth, some research suggests differently. According to an Oxford University study, youth who played video games for less than one hour per day "were associated with the highest levels of sociability and were most likely to say they were satisfied with their lives."[28] The researchers also found that these youth were more well-adjusted than youth who never played video games and youth who played video games for more than three hours per day. According to Andrew Przybylski, who led the study, "If there was a magic dose [of video games], it would be less than one hour. If there was a dangerous dose, it would be more than three hours."[29]

VIOLENT VIDEO GAMES

In a separate Oxford University study, researchers found that the amount of time youth play video games has a greater impact on their behavior than the type of video games they play. Researchers analyzed the video game habits of more than 200 children ages ten and eleven. The study found that found that youth who played video

Experts recommend limiting the amount of time that children play video games. Too much play may negatively affect a child's behavior.

games for less than an hour a day were less likely to have problems with aggression than youth who played no video games.

On the other hand, youth who played video games for more than three hours a day displayed more aggression. The researchers concluded that, "Taken together, this suggests that quantity may play a larger role than the quality of games played."[30]

Whether violent video games inspire actual violent behavior is a hotly debated topic. According to the American Psychological Association (APA), scientists have been looking to the matter for more than two decades. In an official resolution released in 2015, the

APA said there was a correlation between the use of violent video games and aggressive behavior. However, the APA noted that there was "insufficient research" into whether violent video games contributed to acts of "lethal violence."[31]

> **"As with the entertainment of earlier generations, we may look back on some of today's games with nostalgia, and our grandchildren may wonder what all the fuss was about."**[32]
>
> *–Dr. Cheryl Olson, professor of psychiatry at the Harvard Medical School's Center for Mental Health and Media*

Though some critics argue that the advanced graphics in modern video games are more harmful for youth in the long term, other experts such as Dr. Cheryl Olson, a professor of psychiatry at the Harvard Medical School's Center for Mental Health and Media, disagree. "No one has shown a causal link between violent games and real world violent behavior," she said. "As with the entertainment of earlier generations, we may look back on some of today's games with nostalgia, and our grandchildren may wonder what all the fuss was about."[32]

VIDEO GAMES AND MENTAL HEALTH

When most people talk about youth and video games, they focus on whether video games lead to violent behavior. But according to psychologist Jay Hull, "aggression is just the tip of the iceberg."[33] Hull developed a study to see whether video games may increase other negative behaviors in teens. He looked at behaviors such as smoking cigarettes, binge drinking, and unprotected sex. His study found that teens who regularly played violent video games were more likely to engage in risky behaviors. In a previous study, Hull examined violent video game playing and its effect on teens' driving habits. In particular, he looked at video games that encouraged negative behavior. He found that teens who played violent games were more likely to drive recklessly than others. According to Hull, both of his studies showed that video games could affect a teen's personality and their choices.

Video game critics don't just believe video games can lead to aggression or risky behaviors. They also believe video games can affect players' overall mental health. According to Dunckley, excessive video game use has been linked to "depression, anxiety, and hostility."[34] She cited a study that looked at the video game habits of more than 3,000 children over a two-year period. The study found that youth who became compulsive gamers were also more likely to become more depressed and anxious.

However, other studies on youth and video games have found conflicting results. For example, a study from faculty at Columbia University's Mailman School of Public Health found that playing video games may have positive effects on youths' mental health. The study looked at the video game habits of 3,000 children between the ages of six and eleven. It found that youth who played video games for at least five hours a week had fewer psychological problems than those who didn't. Those who played at least five hours of video games were also judged by their teachers as being better students and more socially adjusted than others. According to Katherine Keyes, one of the study's authors, "What we're seeing here is that kids who play a lot of video games are socially integrated, they're prosocial, they

The Nintendo Game Boy revolutionized mobile gaming, allowing youth to play video games in more places and for longer amounts of time. Modern mobile gaming happens on smartphones or on consoles such as the Nintendo Switch.

have good school functioning. And we don't see any association with adverse mental health outcomes."[35]

Video games' effect on youths' social skills is another common cause of concern for parents. But the researchers from the Mailman School of Public Health found that video games were good for youth's social lives. They found links between more video game play and improved peer relationships and social skills. "Video game playing is often a collaborative leisure time activity for school-aged children, and these results indicate that children who frequently play video games may be socially cohesive with peers and integrated into the school community," Keyes said.[36]

As video game technology has evolved, it has created new opportunities for players to interact in person and online. According to a study by the Pew Research Center, 83 percent of teen video game players play with people in person and 75 percent play with people online. The study also found that video games "play an important role in the creation of teens' friendships."[37] This was especially true for teen boys. More than half of the male video gamers surveyed said they had met friends while playing online video games. Teens also play video games online with friends they met in person. As Pew Research Center's study found, "Playing games can have the effect of reinforcing a sense of friendship and connectedness for teens

> **"Playing games can have the effect of reinforcing a sense of friendship and connectedness for teens who play online with friends."[38]**
>
> *–Pew Research Center study*

who play online with friends."[38] Seventy-eight percent of teens who played online video games said they felt "more connected to existing friends they play games with."[39]

VIDEO GAMES AND PHYSICAL HEALTH

As youth spend more time interacting with friends online and through video games, people worry about how screen time is affecting their health. Today's youth spend an average of seven and half hours a day in front of a screen. According to the US Department of Health & Human Services (HHS), a large portion of this time is spent playing video games. It reported that "nearly one-third of high school students play video or computer games for 3 or more hours on an average school day."[40] The World Health Organization (WHO) has said that though there are clear benefits to our society's increasing use of electronic devices, there are drawbacks too. Gregory Hartl, a spokesman for WHO, said that "health problems as a result of excessive use have also been documented."[41] Screen time has been linked to obesity, sleep issues, and eye problems. According to Dunckley, "Like many other aspects of our fast-paced but often sedentary lifestyle, screen-time is introducing new variables into the health equation."[42]

Public health researchers have previously found a link between television viewing among youth and an increased risk of obesity. A 2016 Harvard University study found that the same theory holds true for other youth media use, such as smartphones or video games. According to Dr. Erica Kenney, a public health researcher at Harvard and the lead researcher on the study:

> We have known for years now that spending too much time watching television contributes to a higher risk of developing obesity among kids, mostly because watching too much TV can lead to an unhealthy diet. We see similar associations between other screen device use and diet, physical activity, and obesity risk as we've seen in the past for TV.[43]

The study, published in the *Journal of Pediatrics*, found that teens who spent a minimum of five hours a day using electronic screens, not including televisions, increased their risk of obesity by 43 percent, compared to youth who did not have such heavy screen use.

The study looked at 2013–2015 survey data from nearly 25,000 teens in grades 9 to 12. It found that about one in five teens spent at least five hours a day using screens other than televisions. It also found that an increased use of electronic screen devices was

VIDEO GAMES AS PRESCRIPTIONS

Some people claim video games are bad for children's mental health. But the video game developer Akili Interactive Labs believes video games could have a different effect on youths' mental health problems. It thinks video games could treat those issues. Akili Interactive Labs has developed a video game to treat youth with attention deficit hyperactivity disorder (ADHD). They have plans to seek approval from the Food and Drug Administration, and hope the game will become the first prescription video game.

Akili's video game is designed to be played on a tablet. In it, players float down a lava river through an icy land. Players are rewarded with stars and points as they complete tasks within the game. According to a *Scientific American* article, "Akili sees the video game as the delivery system for targeted algorithms that act as a medical device to activate certain neural networks." Akili CEO Eddie Martucci said the game was designed to target "the key neurological pathways that control attention and impulsivity."

In a study, Akili had 348 children between the ages of eight and twelve who were diagnosed with ADHD play their action-packed game for four weeks. Those who played Akili's game saw improvements in the areas of inhibition control and attention compared to children who were given a different video game. However, the video game hasn't been tested against medications or psychotherapy to see if it is as effective these techniques in managing ADHD.

Quoted in Esther Landhuis, "Companies Seek FDA Approval for Brain Games to Treat ADHD," Scientific American, *November 2, 2015. www.scientificamerican.com.*

linked to the consumption of more sugary beverages and reduced levels of physical activity. But, despite their findings, the study's authors noted that the study does not prove that television or other screen use causes obesity. As writer Lisa Rapaport explained in a *Reuters* article on the study, "It's also possible that excessive screen time was caused by obesity, inactivity or fatigue rather than these things being caused by too much time with TVs, smartphones or tablets."[44] Though this study does not prove that screen use causes obesity, Dr. David L. Hill, a pediatrician and chair of the American Academy of Pediatrics Council on Communications and Media, said it does provide a link between obesity and screen use. He said, "This study helps us understand that the link between obesity and media use may extend to other types of screens."[45]

> "It's also possible that excessive screen time was caused by obesity, inactivity or fatigue rather than these things being caused by too much time with TVs, smartphones or tablets."[44]
>
> –Lisa Rapaport, writer

Hill noted that the link between screen time and obesity may come about because teens using this media see more ads for unhealthy foods and then eat more of them. Or, the link could be caused by a decreased quality of sleep. Hill explained that screen time has been shown to decrease the quality and amount of teens' sleep. Reduced sleep is linked to obesity. Hill said, "We encourage parents to work with kids to examine . . . how much sleep should they get, when should they eat, how much time do they need for homework, exercise, and family activities," Hill said.[46] He believes a conversation about screen time and time management may help the problem. Hill added, "Screen media time should then fit in around those activities or complement them rather than displacing them."[47]

As children spend more and more time engaged with electronic media, they are spending less time being physically active. HHS found that more than 80 percent of US youth don't get the recommended sixty minutes a day of aerobic physical activity. Some argue that video games could be a solution to this problem. A 2015 study by the University of Tennessee Knoxville showed that active video games such as *Wii Sports* or *Kinect Adventures* could be just as beneficial as outdoor play. Over the course of three weeks, child participants "engaged in one active video gaming session and one unstructured outdoor playtime" for twenty-minute sessions.[48] During the sessions the participants wore accelerometers on their hips. The researchers found that "active video gaming [had] a greater percentage of moderate to vigorous intensity than unstructured outdoor play."[49] They concluded that while active gaming shouldn't replace outdoor play entirely, it is a good alternative for occasional play.

VIDEO GAMES AND SLEEP

Video games have also been blamed for youth sleep problems. People's bodies have natural rhythms called biorhythms that control body processes such as hormones and sleep-wake cycles. These rhythms can be affected by natural and artificial light. For example, the bright light of electronic screens can suppress the sleep hormone melatonin. When someone has decreased melatonin levels,

Teens who play video games for long periods of time may stay up too late or skip sleeping entirely. This can negatively affect their physical and mental health.

it may prevent her from entering the deepest phases of the sleep cycle, rapid eye movement (REM) sleep. This can lead to poor sleep quality. According to Lauren Hale, a sleep researcher at Stony Brook University, "As kids . . . use screens, with light shining in their eyes and close to their face, bedtime gets delayed. It takes longer to fall asleep, sleep quality is reduced and total sleep time is decreased."[50]

Hale enforces screen time rules for her children. They are not allowed to look at screens in the hour before their bed time, and no screens are allowed in their bedroom. The message sunk in for her children, as her four-year-old son told a family member: "You don't want to look at a screen before bed because it tells your brain to stay awake."[51]

Though melatonin levels and REM sleep can be thrown off by any type of electronic light, a study found that video games in particular may negatively affect sleep. The study looked at the electronic media habits of more than 2,000 elementary and junior high school youth. Researchers found that it took about two hours of passive electronic screen time, such as watching television, to lead to sleep disturbances. But it only took thirty minutes of interactive electronic screen time, such as playing video games, to cause sleep disturbances.

VIDEO GAMES AND DEVELOPMENT

Critics worry about video games' effects on youth's mental and physical health. They also worry about how games may affect their grades. For example, some people blame video games for what they see as youths' decreasing attention spans. They also argue that the large quantity of video games in education isn't good for students.

On the other hand, some studies have found that young children who play a lot of video games may be better off intellectually than non-gaming youth. A study from the Mailman School of Public Health looked at mental health data for thousands of children between the ages of six and eleven. Researchers found that children who played a lot of video games were "1.88 times more likely to have 'high overall school competence.'"[52] After researchers had accounted for variations in youth's intellectual development, they found that increased video game usage was also linked to a "1.75 times increase in the odds of high intellectual functioning."[53] Despite this, Keyes, one of the survey's

By playing video games with their children, parents can spend time with them as well as monitor the content. This can help keep parents informed.

authors, argued that parents should still set limits on their children's screen time—including video game play. She said it was an important part of a parent's responsibility in terms of "an overall strategy for student success."[54]

PARENTS, YOUTH, AND VIDEO GAMES

As video games and other electronics become an increasingly large part of youth's lives, medical experts are helping parents navigate their children's digital worlds. Dr. Jenny Radesky was the lead author of the American Academy of Pediatrics' guidelines on media and children.

Though Radesky said that both she and her husband spent their childhoods playing video games, they try to do things differently with their sons.

Their children do not use media during the weekdays. When the children are allowed screen time, Radesky tries to limit it to family movie nights. This is part of the "joint media engagement" idea she promotes in her research, which suggests that it is best for parents to share screen time with their kids.[55] On weekends, her children can use apps and play video games like *Minecraft*, but even then, Radesky talks them through the process. "I try to help my older son be aware of the way he reacts to video games or how to interpret information we find online," Radesky said.[56]

> **"I try to help my older son be aware of the way he reacts to video games or how to interpret information we find online."**[56]
>
> –Dr. Jenny Radesky, pediatrician

A study from the ESA found that 90 percent of parents are present when their child either buys or receives a video game, and nine out of ten parents require their child to get their permission before buying a game. It also found that more than 70 percent of parents believe video games have a "positive influence on their child's life."[57] But parents aren't the only ones who have opinions on their children's video games. Since video games heavily influence youth, they also impact society at large.

CHAPTER 3

YOUTH, VIDEO GAMES, AND SOCIETY

For almost as long as there have been video games, politicians, government officials, and scientists have been worrying about their effects on youth. In 1993, Connecticut senator Joe Lieberman held the first federal hearing on violent video games and their effects on youth. This led the video game industry to create the Entertainment Software Ratings Board (ESRB) to rate video games. At least three trained reviewers assign each game a rating based on its content. Almost all video games that are sold carry a rating assigned by the ESRB. The packaging also contains descriptions of the game's content, such as intense violence, blood and gore, or cartoon violence.

There are five ratings assigned to video games: E, E10+, T, M, and AO. The E rating stands for everyone because the game is appropriate for players of all ages. The E rating is similar to the G rating given to children's movies. However, even some of these games include violence. The Harvard Center for Risk Analysis found that of fifty-five games with an E rating, thirty-five had intentional acts of violence. The E10+ rating is given to games which are appropriate for everyone older than ten. Compared to the E rating, E10+ games may contain more violence, as well as slightly suggestive themes. The T rating stands for teen, which means these games are appropriate for teenagers.

Horizon Zero Dawn *was one of the most popular games of 2017. It was assigned a rating of T by the ESRB.*

T-rated games may include suggestive themes, as well as some blood and violence. The M rating stands for mature. These games are recommended for gamers 17 and older. They may include sexual content, strong language, and more violence and gore than games rated for younger players. Video games may also receive an AO rating, which stands for adults only. The AO rating is rarely used. The majority of video games are designed for younger players. According to the ESRB's *2017 Sales, Demographic, and Usage Data Essential Facts* report, of the approximately 1,500 video games which were assigned ratings by the ESRB in 2016, 67 percent were rated E or E10+.

The APA has encouraged the ESRB to further update their ratings to include "the levels and characteristics of violence in games."[58] The ESRB's website does provide ratings summaries of games as well as content descriptors that point out aspects of games parents may not like. For example, the ESRB's page for the E-rated video game *Mario Party 10* has a content descriptor that says the game contains "mild cartoon violence."[59] Its ratings summary tells parents that *Mario Party 10* has games that "depict characters bonking each other with mallets or pushing each other off cloud-like ledges."[60] ERSB's page for the M-rated video game *Call of Duty: Modern Warfare 2*, on the other hand, notes that the game contains drug references, intense violence, language, and blood. The rating summary for *Call of Duty: Modern Warfare 2* also warns parents that in the game, players "kill enemy soldiers throughout the battlefields. Realistic gunfire, explosions, and cries of pain are heard during the frequent and fast-paced combat."[61]

The ESRB's rating system has been found to be more effectively enforced by third-party retailers than the rating system used for movies. The 2011 US Supreme Court ruling made it legal for minors to buy M-rated video games. However, many retailers such as GameStop have their own policies restricting the sale of M-rated video games to people under 17. In 2013, the Federal Trade Commission (FTC) did an undercover survey which found that "the video game industry demonstrated the 'highest level of compliance.'"[62] During the FTC's survey, underage shoppers attempted to buy a video game rated M. Only 13 percent of the shoppers were able to do so—lower than the 24 percent of underage customers who were able to buy a ticket to an R-rated movie in a similar FTC undercover study.

Some people argue that teens who play video games are more likely to commit crimes. Others believe that video games keep youth who might otherwise commit crimes busy.

VIDEO GAMES BLAMED FOR YOUTH CRIME

In the late 1990s, politicians and government officials became concerned about video games' supposed link to violent crime. The issue came to a head in 1999 after the Columbine High School shooting in which two teenagers killed 13 people. In his book *Jacked: The Outlaw Story of Grand Theft Auto*, David Kushner wrote:

> *As the shootings unfolded on TVs around the world, millions of concerned parents desperately tried to make sense of this*

incredibly senseless crime. They needed something to blame,
something controllable, something to assure them that this
would never happen in their families.[63]

The media linked both of the shooters to the video game *Doom*.
Copies of it were found in the shooters' homes, and one of the
shooters mentioned the game in a diary. Victims' families even sued
two dozen video game makers, claiming that violent video games
desensitized the shooters and led to the tragedy. A judge dismissed
the lawsuits, but that was far from the end of the controversy.

Politicians began to blame video games for school shootings.
President Bill Clinton said that video games "make our children
more active participants in simulated violence."[64] He also ordered an
investigation into the advertising practices of violent entertainment.
Republican Newt Gingrich, former Speaker of the House, also blamed
video games and movies for "undermining the core values of civility."[65]
At the time, lawyer and anti-video game activist Jack Thompson
became well-known for his criticism of video games. He claimed that
youth "cannot differentiate between fantasy and reality, so they play
these games and then think if they do the same thing in reality, it's
okay, there will be no consequences."[66]

Despite this criticism, some scholars argue that video games
do not contribute to youth crime. Chris Ferguson, a professor
of psychology who has done research on video game violence,
has said, "There is no good evidence that video games or other
media contributes, even in a small way, to mass homicides or any
other violence among youth."[67] Dr. Patrick Markey, a professor of
psychology at Villanova University, has also argued that though video
games may briefly increase aggression in players, they don't cause
drastic behavior or personality changes. He said that playing a violent

A memorial was built in Littleton, Colorado, for the 13 people who died in the Columbine High School massacre. Critics of video games blamed the shooting on the game Doom.

video game may make a player more likely to have an argument with a sibling, "but playing a violent video game is not going to cause someone to become a school shooter or fundamentally change who they are as an individual."[68]

In 2014, Markey conducted a study that compared violent crime statistics to the release dates of violent video games in series such as Grand Theft Auto and Call of Duty. His research showed a connection between the video game release dates and decreases in violent crime. In the past, researchers have previously found a connection between the release of violent blockbuster movies and drops in violent crime. They think a similar pattern is taking shape with video games.

According to the ESA, men younger than eighteen make up the largest percentage of video game players. Men between the ages of eighteen and thirty-five are the second largest video game consumers. Statistics from the Bureau of Justice Statistics show that men in these age groups are arrested for violent crimes at higher rates that other groups. Ferguson explained the drop in crime rates around the time that violent games are released. He said that video games keep this demographic busy so they're not out in public committing crimes. "We know that violent video game playing in society is correlated with youth violence. It's just in the opposite direction that most people, or most older adults particularly, think that it ought to be," he said.[69]

> **"We know that violent video game playing in society is correlated with youth violence. It's just in the opposite direction that most people, or most older adults particularly, think that it ought to be."[69]**
>
> *–Chris Ferguson, professor*

VIDEO GAME LEGISLATION

After the Columbine High School shooting, local and state governments went to greater lengths to legislate video games. In 2002, US representative Joe Baca introduced the Protect Children from Video Game Sex and Violence Act of 2002. It would have made it illegal to sell M-rated video games to minors if they did not have permission from their parents. At the time, Baca said, "We saw what happened in Columbine. These are kids that are being programmed. They play the video games . . . and they began to commit those particular crimes."[70] Despite Baca's harsh criticism of video games, the act failed to pass.

The following year, Saint Louis county in Missouri attempted to ban the sale of violent video games to youth. The ensuing debate went all the way to the 8th US Circuit Court of Appeals, which ruled against the measure on the basis of the First Amendment. The First Amendment states in part that "Congress shall make no law respecting an establishment of religion, or prohibiting the free exercise thereof; or abridging the freedom of speech, or of the press."[71] The 8th US Circuit Court of Appeals wrote that if the First Amendment was versatile enough to protect the work of famous artists, musicians and authors, they saw "no reason why . . . video games are not entitled to similar protection."[72]

Despite the failure of this legislation, in 2005 the state of California also attempted to restrict the sale of violent video games to youth. The California law banned retailers from selling or renting violent video games to minors. The law was controversial. The case, known as *Brown v. Entertainment Merchants Association*, went all the way to the US Supreme Court in November 2010. At the hearing, the California Attorney General argued that the law was necessary because of the "deviant level of violence that is presented in a certain category of video games."[73] The Supreme Court disagreed. In a 7-2 decision, the Supreme Court struck down the law. Once again, it argued that video games were protected by the First Amendment.

Conservative Supreme Court justice Antonin Scalia wrote that: "Like the protected books, plays and movies that preceded them, video games communicate ideas—and even social messages. . . . That suffices to confer First Amendment rights."[74]

The Supreme Court also rejected the idea that video game violence inspires players to commit violent acts. Justice Scalia wrote that "psychological studies purporting to show a connection between exposure to violent video games and harmful effects on children do not prove that such exposure causes minors to act aggressively."[75] This decision by the Supreme Court would make it more difficult for local, state, and federal governments to legislate the video games industry going forward.

In the years that followed, video games have remained a common topic of conversation for politicians, particularly after tragedies such as school shootings. For example, after the Parkland, Florida, school shooting, President Donald Trump held a meeting to look at the supposed links between violent video games and mass shootings. Many Republican lawmakers and media commentators had urged Trump to put new restrictions on how youth could purchase

> **"Like the protected books, plays and movies that preceded them, video games communicate ideas—and even social messages. . . . That suffices to confer First Amendment rights."[74]**
>
> *—Antonin Scalia,*
> *Supreme Court justice*

violent video games. Representatives from the video game industry also attended the meeting. After the meeting, the ESA released a statement about what its representatives had contributed: "We discussed the numerous scientific studies establishing that there is no connection between video games and violence, First Amendment protection of video games, and how our industry's rating system effectively helps parents make informed entertainment choices," they wrote.[76]

> **"We discussed the numerous scientific studies establishing that there is no connection between video games and violence, First Amendment protection of video games, and how our industry's rating system effectively helps parents make informed entertainment choices."** [76]
>
> –the ESA

VIDEO GAMES AND ADDICTION

Politicians and government officials are also concerned that video games can lead youth to addiction. Former US Surgeon General C. Everett Koop commented that he was worried teenagers were becoming addicted to video games "body and soul."[77] Though most addictions are caused by substances, video game addiction would be considered an arousal addiction. According to Dunckley, this means that players can become addicted to the "high levels of stimulation and arousal" in video games.[78]

Some video game supporters argue that players get hooked on video games for a much simpler reason: they enjoy them. In his book, *Everything Bad is Good for You*, Steven Johnson wrote: "Most of the time, when you're hooked on a game, what draws you in is an elemental form of desire: the desire to *see the next thing*."[79] He argues that it's similar to the what people feel when they are absorbed in entertaining movies or television shows. However, Johnson notes that video games are different in one important way. Players get to decide how the game progresses.

Medical experts and scholars are also divided as to whether video game addiction can be considered a true disorder. But in June 2018, WHO listed "gaming disorder" as a mental health condition in its International Classification of Diseases (ICD) for the first time. Since gaming disorder is now included in the ICD, doctors can diagnosis it as an addiction, prescribe treatment, and get patients' insurance to pay for it. Dr. Vladimir Poznyak, a member of WHO's Department of Mental Health and Substance Abuse, said that since gaming disorder is now in the ICD, health care professionals will be "alerted to the existence of this condition." He added, "people who suffer from these conditions can get appropriate help."[80]

In order to be diagnosed with gaming disorder, an individual must prioritize gaming over other activities, be unable to control this behavior, and be negatively affected by this behavior but continue doing it anyway. An individual must experience these symptoms for twelve months. "It cannot be just an episode of few hours or few days," Poznyak explained.[81] Though millions of people around the world play video games, Poznyak noted that "Millions of gamers around the world, even when it comes to the intense gaming, would never qualify as people suffering from gaming disorder."[82] He added that gamers have a low chance of developing gaming disorder.

In 2018, Douglas Gentile, Iowa State psychology professor, estimated that about three million US children could be addicted to gaming. He stressed that it's not the amount of time youth spend playing video games that matters, it's "whether they are continuing to game despite increasingly negative effects on their life." Gentile added, "Most kids don't have a problem. . . . But given how prevalent gaming is, even if it's a small percentage that do have a problem, it's still a lot of kids."[83] When he started studying video games and their effects in 1999, Gentile did not believe that children could get addicted to gaming. But, in recent years, his opinion has changed. He said, "I didn't believe it could be a real problem back then, but the

YOUTH VIDEO GAME ADDICTION IN OTHER COUNTRIES

When WHO included gaming disorder in the ICD, there was speculation that it had been pressured to do so by representatives from countries in Asia. About 10 to 15 percent of young people in countries in Asia are believed to suffer from gaming disorder. In western countries that number is believed to be between 1 and 10 percent. In South Korea and China, for example, young men average about forty hours a week of video game play.

To combat the issue, South Korea and China restrict minors' video game use by creating curfews at internet cafes. Online games in South Korea and China also have added in "fatigue systems" which are designed to encourage players to stop playing after a certain number of hours. These systems, which are built into the games, reduce the number of awards players receive after a set amount of time. In 2011, South Korea also passed a law that affected youth's video game play in their own homes. The law banned youth under the age of 16 from playing online games between the hours of midnight and six o'clock in the morning. In 2014, South Korea amended the law to allow parents to lift the ban on their own children.

more I studied it, the more I realized that in some kids, it can rise [to an addiction]."[84] Now that gaming disorder has an official diagnosis by WHO, Gentile believes that it will lead to more research on the subject as well as better treatment options.

The majority of treatments for gaming disorder are based on cognitive behavioral therapy. This is a type of therapy in which patients talk with a mental health counselor. Other treatment options for gaming disorder include family therapy, in which family members meet with a professional to help them better communicate and manage conflicts; motivational interviews, where parents and family members help the patient set progress goals and work toward them; and support groups. The self-help group Online Gamers Anonymous provides gamers with a 12-step recovery program similar to the one used by Alcoholics Anonymous. "Having a support group is always a good idea and treating it like an addiction is the best strategy that we know of," said pediatrician Dr. Amy Shriver.[85]

> **"Having a support group is always a good idea and treating it like an addiction is the best strategy that we know of."[85]**
>
> *–Dr. Amy Shriver, pediatrician*

As part of the treatment of gaming disorder, medical professionals may also look at what is causing the youth to play video games so frequently. "Sometimes gaming overuse can be a symptom that something is going wrong for the child," said Christopher Ferguson.[86] Heather Senior Monroe, director of program development at Newport Academy, which operates treatment centers for youth with mental health issues, agrees with Ferguson. She said that in many cases, health professionals are more focused on what is causing the excessive video game use than the excessive video game use itself. According to Monroe, "The behavior is like any other self-harming behavior—a way to escape reality. The treatment is then about why. Why does that person want to escape their reality so much?"[87] Monroe stated that common reasons include depression and anxiety.

VIDEO GAMES IN EDUCATION

As health experts and scholars worry about video game addiction, video game supporters are actively making video games a larger part of youth's lives. This is especially true in the field of education. According to author Jane McGonigal, when educational games work well, they "provide a welcome relief to students who otherwise feel under engaged in their daily school lives."[88] But McGonigal and other video game supporters believe a more dramatic approach is needed. For example, author Marc Prensky suggested an ideal school wouldn't just use games to educate students. In his book *Don't Bother Me Mom—I'm Learning,* Prensky states that schools would benefit from using strategies based on ones that make games so engaging.

That dream has become a reality with Quest to Learn, a public school for students in grades 6 through 12 that brings the video game experience into the classroom. The school is the first game-based school in the world, but its founders hope it's not the last. Quest to Learn opened in 2009. The school is run by a partnership of professional educators and video game designers. The school's curriculum is developed by Katie Salen, a video game expert who has studied how youth learn through games.

In some ways, the curriculum at Quest to Learn is like that of other schools. Students learn traditional subjects like science, English,

Quest to Learn students have classes with many interactive opportunities. Teacher Leach Hirsch (right) shows students a visual model of DNA.

history, geography, and foreign languages. But they are taught these subjects in different ways. At Quest to Learn, students take classes such as Codeworlds, which is a hybrid of math and English. These courses use video game techniques to keep students more engaged. Jane McGonigal writes that Quest to Learn students "are engaged in gameful activities from the moment they wake up in the morning to the moment they finish their final homework assignment at night."[89] For example, students at Quest to Learn don't have assignments, they have "secret missions." These include assignments that are hidden in books in the school library. "Having a secret mission means you're not learning and practicing fractions because you have to do it," McGonigal wrote. "You're working toward a self-chosen goal."[90]

Students at Quest to Learn also don't work for grades like students at traditional schools. Instead, they "level up." As in a game, students work on projects or assignments to earn points. McGonigal notes that "leveling up" is in many ways a fairer form of measurement than traditional grades. "Everyone can level up, as long as they keep working hard," she wrote.[91] This system may also be less stressful for students because they work to earn points, not to avoid bad grades. This replaces negative stress with positive stress.

Video game supporters are happy to see the tactics being used at Quest to Learn. "It's too early to say how this approach will affect future performance but seeing new world skills front and center in the classroom is an encouraging sign," wrote author Aaron Dignan.[92] Like many video game experts and game designers, Dignan believes video games will only become a bigger part of everyone's lives in the future, including those of youth.

> **"Everyone can level up, as long as they keep working hard."**[91]
>
> –Jane McGonigal, author of Reality Is Broken

THE FUTURE OF YOUTH AND VIDEO GAMES

In their book *Got Game: How the Gamer Generation is Reshaping Business Forever,* John C. Beck and Mitchell Wade write that "for today's young adults, and the many millions coming along behind them, games are much more than any fad. For one thing, they're far more pervasive."[93]

Video game developers and experts expect this trend to continue in years to come. Jane McGonigal predicts that in the future there will be video games designed to increase people's career satisfaction; fix educational systems; treat conditions such as depression, anxiety, and obesity; better engage the elderly; increase democratic participation; and solve worldwide problems like climate change or poverty. "In short," she wrote, "I foresee games that . . . empower us to change the world in meaningful ways."[94]

McGonigal is not alone in these predictions. Aaron Dignan also envisions a world where video games are more ingrained in people's daily lives. Dignan predicts the principles of video game design will be incorporated into school systems and government organizations. He wrote, "Can you imagine a world where our most basic activities are even half as enjoyable as our favorite games? Where every ounce of learning is due to play rather than at its expense. That world

As of 2018, more than 3.4 million people played Fortnite. *Many of these players were children and teens.*

can be made real, one game at a time."[95] Video game designers believe a world like this is possible because of our increasing use of technologies such as GPS, biometric devices (which track things such as heart rates), and motion sensors. McGonigal said the more people engage with these technologies, "the more we'll be able to chart our progress, set goals, accept challenges, and support each other in our real lives in the way we do in our best games."[96] This future is also made more possible through society's increasing use of mobile devices.

Youth are using mobile devices more and more. According to a 2017 report by Common Sense Media, "Children 8 and younger spent about 15 minutes a day staring at a mobile screen in 2013 and now they spend 48 minutes a day."[97] Increasingly, many young people also own smartphones or tablets. The report found that 42 percent of children eight years old or younger have their own tablet devices, compared to 7 percent of children who owned these devices in 2013 and 1 percent who owned them in 2011.

Gentile also believes youth will become increasingly influenced by mobile media. "More and more of our media consumption is on something that is hand-held or back in a child's bedroom where parents are less able to monitor it and set consistent rules," he wrote.[98] For example, a study found that youth aged eight to eleven who had their own televisions or video games in their bedrooms spent more time with media than youth who did not have devices in their bedrooms. This increased media use was associated with reduced sleep and time spent reading, as well as lower grades in school. Gentile said to deal with these issues, it's important for parents to find the appropriate balance of screen and media use for their children. But, he explained, that perfect balance is hard to find:

> **"More and more of our media consumption is on something that is hand-held or back in a child's bedroom where parents are less able to monitor it and set consistent rules."**[98]
>
> –Douglas Gentile, professor

As a society we haven't really figured out where that is . . . because children's media screen time generally just keeps going up and up every time we measure it. And there's not going to be a one-size-fits-all answer.[99]

THE FUTURE OF ALTERNATE REALITY

As the ways that youth access electronic media and video games change, so do the types of video games that are available to them. New technologies such as AR, alternate reality games (ARGs), and virtual reality (VR) are changing the way youth are able to interact with video games and the world around them. AR technology introduces a layer of real world content or information into video game play. Many people were first exposed to this technology in the game *Pokémon Go*. With the increasing number of smartphones in use today, Dignan has suggested that AR games are a "fertile territory for the future of gaming."[100]

Like AR games, alternate reality games (ARGs) blend the real and virtual worlds. As writer Eric Thrum said in *Wired,* "An [ARG] is, more or less, exactly what it sounds like: a constructed world with a fictional history that layers on top of the "real" world."[101] According to McGonigal, "ARGs are games you play to get more out of your real life, as opposed to games you play to escape it."[102]

There are three main types of ARGs: life-management ARGs, concept ARGs, and organizational ARGs. *Chore Wars* is an example of a life-management ARG because it helps players approach their real-life tasks as though they are objectives in a game. *Chore Wars* is based on MMOs like *World of Warcraft*. But it is designed to be played in the real world. Rather than completing online quests, players earn points by completing real-world chores. Each chore someone completes in the real world earns their *Chore Wars'* avatar rewards such as treasure, power-ups, or points to increase their skill levels.

SuperBetter is a concept ARG. It is a superhero-themed game that was designed to help people deal with health problems such as recovering from an injury or managing a chronic condition. It allows

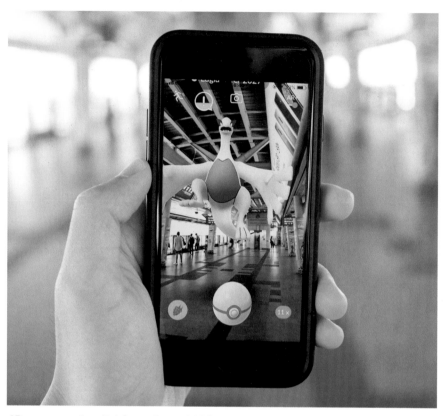

AR games such as Pokémon Go *and ARGs may be the future of video games. Players will be able to interact with fictional characters in the real world and real elements in a fictional world.*

players to share game ideas, missions, and rules that other players can adapt in their own lives. In *SuperBetter*, players create a secret identity, complete missions, and recruit real-world allies who help keep track of the players' progress in the game.

Organizational ARGs use video game design to create change in institutions and organizations. McGonigal classifies the video-game-inspired school Quest to Learn as one type of organizational ARG. Students complete quests instead of homework assignments and level up instead of receiving grades.

THE FUTURE OF YOUTH AND VIRTUAL REALITY

With VR technology, people use a headset that appears to transport them into three-dimensional, digital worlds. VR became increasingly popular in late 2017. More than one million VR headsets were shipped during the third quarter of the year. Facebook and YouTube tried to capitalize on the trend by creating 360-degree videos. Gamers started playing *Call of Duty* on VR headsets.

However, as the VR industry rapidly expanded, psychologists worried about its potentially dangerous effects, especially on youth. Mark Mon-Williams, a professor of cognitive psychology at Leeds University, said it's important that the VR industry places as much attention on youth safety as it does in creating faster or better products. "There needs to be an understanding of how children interact with a virtual world: how they focus on objects and how they make sense of distances in that world. The crucial point is that we should tackle these problems now," he said.[103]

Scientists at Leeds University hypothesized that prolonged use of VR headsets, especially by children, could lead to vision and balance problems. In their study, twenty children between the ages of eight and twelve were asked to play a twenty-minute VR game and then were examined after. None of the children showed a serious reduction in eyesight, but two children saw decreases in their ability to determine distances. All of these symptoms were short-lived. Faisal Mushtaq, an expert in human performance research who led the study, noted that studies of this kind are important as VR technology becomes more common. "Establishing the scientific evidence base on safe usage is important if we want to ensure that children benefit from all the exciting possibilities that VR has to offer," he said.[104]

Mushtaq said the Leeds study was one of the "first ever investigations into the impact of VR use on children's vision and balance."[105] It's also one of the first to look at the overall effects of VR on its users.

Scientists believe much more of this research is needed to adequately understand the effects of VR on adults and especially children. Marientina Gotsis, an associate professor of research at the Interactive Media and Games Division of the University of Southern California, said that most of the VR headsets on the market today have had little research. The research that has been done primarily looked at young adults. For that reason, Gotsis thinks people with young children should be especially careful with VR. She said that if young children do use VR devices, parents should keep their exposure short. "Children may not know how to communicate discomfort of any sort, such as visual discomfort or motion sickness, so you don't want prolonged exposure on screen," she said.[106]

For that reason, in 2018, most major VR headset manufacturers recommend that youth under age thirteen do not use their devices. Though HTC's VR device Vive doesn't mention a specific age limit, it does say that it's not "designed to be used by children."[107] Likewise, Google's Cardboard doesn't list an age limit, but it says it should only be used with adult supervision. Walter Greenleaf, a Stanford behavioral neuroscientist, believes this is good advice for parents to follow with their children. He also thinks parents should be concerned about VR use themselves. He said that until there is more VR research, he urges everyone to monitor their VR use. He said, "I would be concerned for everyone who uses this. You don't have to have a young brain to have an impact."[108]

VR CONTENT AND YOUTHS' PERCEPTION OF REALITY

A 2017 study funded by Sesame Workshop looked at how VR affected children's memory and their perception of reality. In the study, 55 children between the ages of four and six played a game with the *Sesame Street* character Grover. Half of the children interacted with the character by watching him on TV. The other half saw him through VR. The ones who saw Grover in VR "saw him as more real," said Jeremy Bailenson, director of Stanford's Virtual Human Interaction Lab.

This topic has been researched for almost ten years. A 2009 study showed that children may be more likely than older VR users to see their VR experiences as real. Researchers had young elementary school children watch a virtual version of themselves swim with orcas. A week later when they were asked about their experience, the children said their VR experience was real. To avoid this type of confusion, researchers urge parents to closely monitor their children's VR usage and talk them through the experience. According to Bailenson, "Parents need to be careful, active and participating, because the VR medium is more powerful than traditional media. But with proper adult supervision, using it infrequently, I think it's going to turn out to be just fine."

Quoted in Sandee LaMotte, "The Very Real Health Dangers of Virtual Reality," CNN, December 13, 2017. www.cnn.com.

THE FUTURE OF VIDEO GAME LEGISLATION

For as long as there have been video games, politicians have tried to regulate their use by youth. During the days of video game arcades, politicians were concerned that youth were wasting their quarters on video games. Today, politicians are concerned that youth are spending far more money on modern video game features known as loot boxes. These are essentially digital treasure chests within video games that can provide players with upgrades such as better weapons or different outfits for their avatars. Players can open some loot boxes for free, while other loot boxes can be purchased. For example, in the video game *Overwatch*, players can purchase two loot boxes for $2 or a package of 50 loot boxes for $40. The contents of these loot boxes are randomly generated, so players don't really know what they're buying.

Though loot boxes have been a feature of video games for several years, they made the news in 2017 because of their controversial use in the video game *Star Wars Battlefront II*. In this video game, players had to play for an extended number of hours in order to unlock popular characters such as Luke Skywalker or Darth Vader. However, they could also pay to open loot boxes in the hopes of unlocking them that way. This frustrated players and led to legislation from Hawaiian state representatives Chris Lee and Sean Quinlan. In order to better protect underage players from these practices, Lee and Quinlan developed legislation that targeted loot boxes. Quinlan stressed that loot box regulation was different from previous attempts by the government to regulate video games:

> When I was a teenager, a senator by the name of Joseph Lieberman tried to regulate the content of violent video games. His attempts to conflate video game violence with real world violence did lasting damage to the image of video games and certain publishers. I want to make it clear that we are only regulating a mechanism, not the content of the game itself.[109]

No longer believing that the video game industry would self-regulate these practices, Quinlan agreed to the legislation. "If even mature and intelligent adults are falling victim to these mechanisms, how are kids expected to respond?" Quinlan asked.[110]

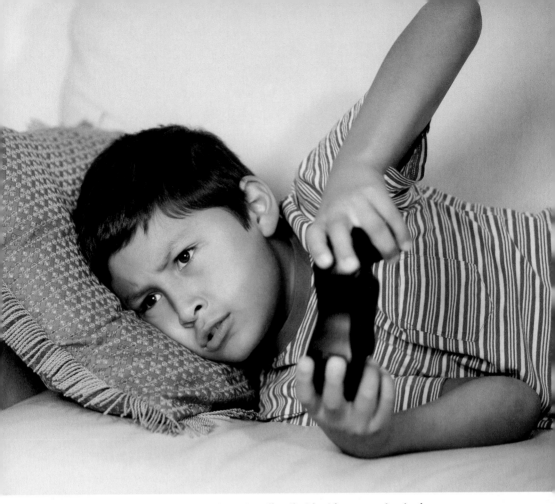

Children who play video games may not realize that loot boxes cost actual money. Some legislators are working on bills to restrict the sale of loot boxes to minors.

Lee was also a video game fan, but he decided something needed to be done to address changes in the video game industry and its effects on youth. He said, "I grew up playing games my whole life. I've watched firsthand the evolution of the industry from one that seeks to create new things to one that's begun to exploit people, especially children, to maximize profit."[111]

Lee and Quinlan introduced a series of four bills targeting loot boxes to the Hawaiian state legislature in January 2018. Two of the bills, HB 2686 and SB 3024, would have banned anyone younger than twenty-one years old from buying video games that allow players to purchase randomized rewards. The other bills, HB 2727 and SB 3025, would have required video game publishers to clearly label games that have randomized purchase systems like loot boxes. It would have also required game publishers to share players' probability of getting each loot box reward. None of the bills became law before the Hawaii State legislature adjourned for the 2018 session in May 2018.

Similar legislation was proposed in the Washington State legislature by state senator Kevin Ranker. SB 6266, introduced in January 2018, would have ordered the Washington State Gambling Commission to investigate loot boxes. According to Ranker, "What the bill says is, 'Industry, state: sit down to figure out the best way to regulate this.' It is unacceptable to be targeting our children with predatory gambling masked in a game with dancing bunnies or something."[112] Since Ranker believed loot boxes looked like gambling, he wanted them regulated like gambling. He also wanted game developers to publicly state the odds of receiving various types of prizes in loot boxes. Ranker said these regulations, among others, would help protect young game players who might not be able to "tell the difference between game play and credit card spending."[113]

Ranker's bill would have asked the Washington State

> "It is unacceptable to be targeting our children with predatory gambling masked in a game with dancing bunnies or something." [112]
>
> –Kevin Ranker, Washington senator

Gambling Commission to determine, among other things, whether these games are considered gambling under Washington law, and whether young game players should have access to them. It also asked the commission to look into the probability of various rewards in loot boxes. Ranker's legislation, however, met the same fate as Lee and Quinlan's. The bill was still in a legislative committee when the Washington state legislature adjourned for the session in March 2018.

Additionally, in 2018 Maryland announced legislation that would require the state's Department of Education and Health Department to create health and safety guidelines on digital media in schools. This bill could make Maryland the first state to tackle parents' worries about youths' increasing screen time in the classroom. According to the market research firm International Data Corporation, in 2017, US primary and secondary schools spent "$5.4 billion on 12.4 million laptop and tablet computers."[114]

As school districts have adopted more electronic learning tools, parents and health experts have become more concerned about how they are affecting youth. Some believe that learning apps with reward systems similar to video games are particularly problematic. Dr. Scott Krugman, a pediatrician who supports legislation on digital devices in classrooms, said that many people are worried these tools are too entertainment-based and not focused enough on education. "We felt these are things that should be tracked and monitored," he said.[115]

THE FUTURE OF VIDEO GAMES IN EDUCATION

Dr. David L. Hill is a pediatrician in Wilmington, North Carolina. He is also the chairman of the American Academy of Pediatrics' council on communications and media. Though the American Academy of Pediatrics has released at-home guidelines for youth and digital media, it hasn't done the same for schools. Hill said that is because the use of electronic devices in schools hasn't been studied enough. Maryland's legislation could help provide more data.

While health experts, legislators, and parents debate the merits of video games in the classroom, others firmly believe in their benefits. Writer Christina Beck states that "far from rotting brains, video games challenge both children and adults to think differently and more creatively."[116] Numerous studies have backed up these claims, as video games have been proven to be capable of teaching substantive subjects while improving student engagement. Many experts in the fields of education and computer science also argue that it's important for today's youth to interact well with digital worlds that will become a bigger part of their lives in the future.

With that in mind, more digital learning tools are entering youth's classrooms. Video game developer Immersed Games is working on an educational video game, *Tyto Online*, that engages players in the same way as *World of Warcraft*. Lindsey Tropf, the CEO and founder of Immersed Games, said that *Tyto Online* is designed to provide the same entertainment benefits as a traditional MMO. "We're creating a game that teaches but also plays like a real game—because it is," she said.[117] Traditional MMO roleplaying games (MMORPGs) are filled with quests and raids, and *Tyto Online* players face similar challenges. They're just designed to be educational. According to Tropf, "Instead of killing boars and collecting hides for quests, you're doing things like looking for evidence about if something is an invasive species that you can then transplant out and save the local ecosystem."[118]

Some video games even teach players to code. These games can be used in various classes to foster an interest in science, technology, engineering, and math (STEM). Popular video games such as *Minecraft* allow players to input code to change aspects of the game. By entering console commands, *Minecraft* players can enchant items, clone groups of blocks, change the game's difficulty level, gain experience points, and even change the weather in the game. To enter a console command or code, players hit the forward-slash key (/). This makes a small window appear. Players input code to activate commands. If players wanted to change the weather within a *Minecraft* game, they would type "/weather" followed by the kind of weather they want, such as "thunder." The "/weather thunder" command would then create a thunderstorm in their games. Children who learn how to code using these games may pursue careers in STEM fields.

In addition to entertainment video games that teach children how to code, there is a growing number of free,

> **"Instead of killing boars and collecting hides for quests, you're doing things like looking for evidence about if something is an invasive species that you can then transplant out and save the local ecosystem."** [118]
>
> *–Lindsey Tropf, CEO and founder of Immersed Games*

online resources that teach youth how to code their own websites, apps, and video games. For example, Code.org offers a variety of courses for all age and skill levels. Youth can also create their own video games, animations, and interactive stories at the MIT Media

Games such as Minecraft *can teach players how to code. This can help them in future programming classes or jobs.*

Lab website. Scratch is a free programming language developed by the Lifelong Kindergarten Group. It was developed primarily for youth between the ages of eight and sixteen. According to journalist Rhett Allain, "It's pretty easy to pick up and it's built so that you can share programs and modify others."[119]

HOW YOUTH AFFECT VIDEO GAMES

Youth aren't just creating video games using Scratch or Code.org. Some youth are making video games professionally. Alex Balfanz, an eighteen-year-old student at Duke University, has made seven-figure profits from a cops-and-robbers adventure video game he created called *Jailbreak*. Other youth are finding success in the video game world as professional E-Sports athletes. For example, 19-year-old Sumail Hassan has made more than $2.5 million playing video games. As of 2018, he is the youngest person to win $1 million in the growing E-Sports industry.

People who grew up in the digital age are making video games their own. They're learning how to make games themselves, excelling at the games they play, and making money doing it. Today, video games are a part of youth's lives, their educations, and in some cases, their careers. And in the future, this trend is expected to continue. Some people argue that video games' increasing influence is bad for youth. Others, like Jane McGonigal believe it's good for everyone. She writes:

Games aren't leading us to the downfall of civilization. They're leading us to its reinvention. The great challenge for us today, and for the remainder of the century, is to integrate games more closely into our everyday lives.[120]

"Games aren't leading us to the downfall of civilization. They're leading us to its reinvention."[120]
–Jane McGonigal, author of Reality Is Broken

SOURCE NOTES

INTRODUCTION: REACHING YOUTH

1. Quoted in Clive Thompson, "The Minecraft Generation," *New York Times*, April 14, 2016. www.nytimes.com.

2. Quoted in Christina Beck, "With MinecraftEdu, Are Video Games the Future of Education?" *Christian Science Monitor*, January 20, 2016. www.csmonitor.com.

3. Quoted in John C. Beck and Mitchell Wade, *Got Game: How the Gamer Generation Is Reshaping Business Forever.* Cambridge, MA: Harvard Business Publishing, 2004, p. 35

4. Quoted in Natasha Singer, "Maryland Schools May Tell Children When It's Time to Log Off," *New York Times*, April 18, 2018. www.nytimes.com.

5. Victoria L. Dunckley, *Reset Your Child's Brain.* San Francisco, CA: New World Library, 2015, p. 69.

6. Marc Prensky, *Don't Bother Me Mom—I'm Learning.* St. Paul, MN: Paragon House, 2006, p. xvii.

7. Quoted in Thompson, "The Minecraft Generation."

CHAPTER 1: HOW DO YOUTH USE VIDEO GAMES?

8. Aaron Dignan, *Game Frame: Using Games as a Strategy for Success.* New York: Free Press, 2011, p. 42.

9. Dignan, *Game Frame*, p. 42.

10. Dignan, *Game Frame*, p. 51.

11. Dignan, *Game Frame*, p. 51.

12. Jane McGonigal, *Reality Is Broken: Why Games Make Us Better and How They Can Change the World.* New York: Penguin, 2011, p. 20.

13. McGonigal, *Reality Is Broken,* p. 30.

14. Quoted in McGonigal, *Reality Is Broken*, p. 11.

15. Quoted in Michael Z. Newman, "Children of the '80s Never Fear: Video Games Did Not Ruin Your Life," *Smithsonian.com*, May 25, 2017. www.smithsonianmag.com.

16. Dignan, *Game Frame*, p. 14.

17. Newman, "Children of the '80s Never Fear."

18. Newman, "Children of the '80s Never Fear."

19. Leo Kelion, "Sega v Nintendo: Sonic, Mario and the 1990's Console War," *BBC News*, May 13, 2014. www.bbc.com.

20. David Kushner, *Jacked: The Outlaw Story of Grand Theft Auto.* Hoboken, NJ: John Wiley & Sons, 2012, p. 16.

21. Kat Eschner, "How 'Mortal Kombat' Changed Video Games," *Smithsonian.com*, September 13, 2017. www.smithsonianmag.com.

22. Kat Eschner, "How 'Mortal Kombat' Changed Video Games."

23. JV Chamary, "Why 'Pokémon GO' Is The World's Most Important Game." *Forbes.com*, February 10, 2018. www.forbes.com.

24. Katia Moskvitch, "The Business Secrets Behind Fortnite's Runaway Success," *Wired*, July 10, 2018. www.wired.co.uk.

25. Moskvitch, "The Business Secrets Behind Fortnite's Runaway Success."

26. Sam Haysom, "Is 'Fortnite' Addiction Among Young Children Actually a Real Problem?" *Mashable*, 29 June 2018. www.mashable.com.

27. Dignan, *Game Frame*, p. 14.

CHAPTER 2: HOW DO VIDEO GAMES AFFECT YOUTH?

28. Quoted in "Video Games Can Be Good for Kids, Study Finds," *CBS News*, August 4, 2014. www.cbsnews.com.

29. Quoted in Nicholas St. Fleur, "Playing Video Games Can Help or Hurt, Depending on Whom You Ask," *NPR*, August 8, 2014. www.npr.org.

30. John Bingham, "Study Finds No Evidence Violent Video Games Make Children Aggressive," *Telegraph*, April 1, 2015. www.telegraph.co.uk.

31. "Resolution on Violent Video Games," *American Psychological Association*, 2015. www.apa.org.

32. Kushner, *Jacked: The Outlaw Story of Grand Theft Auto*, p. 273.

33. St. Fleur, "Playing Video Games Can Help or Hurt, Depending on Whom You Ask."

34. Dunckley, *Reset Your Child's Brain*, p. 58.

35. "Study: Video Games Don't Cause Psychological Harm in Children," *U.S. News & World Report*, March 14, 2016. www.usnews.com.

36. Doug Bolton, "Video Games May Improve Children's Intellectual and Social Skills, Study Finds," *Independent*, March 9, 2016. www.independent.co.uk.

37. Amanda Lenhart, "Chapter 3: Video Games Are Key Elements in Friendships for Many Boys," *Pew Research Center*, August 6, 2015. www.pewinternet.org.

38. Lenhart, "Chapter 3: Video Games Are Key Elements in Friendships for Many Boys."

39. Lenhart, "Chapter 3: Video Games Are Key Elements in Friendships for Many Boys."

40. "Facts & Statistics," *Department of Health and Human Services*, January 26, 2017. www.hhs.gov.

41. Susan Scutti, "WHO to Recognize Gaming Disorder as Mental Health Condition in 2018," *CNN*, December 27, 2017. www.cnn.com.

42. Dunckley, *Reset Your Child's Brain*, p. 20.

43. Lisa Rapaport, "Lots of Teen Screen Time Tied to Obesity," *Reuters*, December 16, 2016. www.reuters.com.

44. Rapaport, "Lots of Teen Screen Time Tied to Obesity."

45. Rapaport, "Lots of Teen Screen Time Tied to Obesity."

46. Rapaport, "Lots of Teen Screen Time Tied to Obesity."

47. Rapaport, "Lots of Teen Screen Time Tied to Obesity."

48. John Biggs, "Study Finds That Active Video Gaming May Be as Good for Kids as Playing Outside," *Tech Crunch*, June 15, 2015. www.techcrunch.com.

49. Biggs, "Study Finds That Active Video Gaming May Be as Good for Kids as Playing Outside."

50. Anya Kamenetz, "What the Screen Time Experts Do with Their Own Kids," *NPR*, February 6, 2018. www.npr.org.

51. Kamenetz, "What the Screen Time Experts Do with Their Own Kids."

52. Bolton, "Video Games May Improve Children's Intellectual and Social Skills."

53. Bolton, "Video Games May Improve Children's Intellectual and Social Skills."

54. Bolton, "Video Games May Improve Children's Intellectual and Social Skills."

55. Kamenetz, "What the Screen Time Experts Do with Their Own Kids."

56. Kamenetz, "What the Screen Time Experts Do with Their Own Kids."

57. "2017 Sales, Demographic, and Usage Data," *Entertainment Software Association*, April 2017. www.theesa.com.

CHAPTER 3: YOUTH, VIDEO GAMES, AND SOCIETY

58. "Resolution on Violent Video Games," *American Psychological Association*, 2015. www.apa.org.

59. "Mario Party 10," *Entertainment Software Rating Board*, n.d. www.esrb.org.

60. "Mario Party 10."

61. "Call of Duty: Modern Warfare 2," *Entertainment Software Rating Board*, n.d. www.esrb.org.

62. Brett Molina and Mike Snider, "Trump Slams Violent Video Games. For Parents, Ratings Should Just Be a Start," *USA Today*, March 12, 2018. www.usatoday.com.

63. Kushner, *Jacked: The Outlaw Story of Grand Theft Auto*, p. 62.

64. Kevin Breuninger, "Trump Linked Video Games and Gun Violence—But Don't Expect Him or Congress to Do Anything About It," *CNBC*, March 9, 2018. www.cnbc.com.

65. Breuninger, "Trump Linked Video Games and Gun Violence."

66. Kushner, *Jacked: The Outlaw Story of Grand Theft Auto*, p. 144

67. Chris Morris, "Trump's Video Game Violence Theory Is Not Supported by the Supreme Court or Researchers," *Fortune*, February 23, 2018. www.fortune.com.

68. Lucy Diavolo, "Following Trump's Meeting on Violent Video Games, Experts Explain What the Research Really Shows," *TeenVogue*, March 14, 2018. www.teenvogue.com.

69. Diavolo, "Following Trump's Meeting on Violent Video Games, Experts Explain What the Research Really Shows."

70. Kushner, *Jacked: The Outlaw Story of Grand Theft Auto*, p. 105.

71. "U.S. Constitution: First Amendment," *Cornell Law School Legal Information Institute*. www.law.cornell.edu.

72. Kushner, *Jacked: The Outlaw Story of Grand Theft Auto*, p. 146.

73. Kushner, *Jacked: The Outlaw Story of Grand Theft Auto*, p. 274.

74. Kushner, *Jacked: The Outlaw Story of Grand Theft Auto*, p. 274.

75. Maya Salam and Liam Stack, "Do Video Games Lead to Mass Shootings? Researchers Say No," *New York Times*, February 23, 2018. www.nytimes.com.

76. Tony Romm, "Inside Trump's Private Meeting with the Video-Game Industry—And Its Critics," *Washington Post*, March 8, 2018. www.washingtonpost.com.

77. Simon Parkin, "Donald Trump Takes On the Nonexistent Link Between Violent Video Games and Mass Shootings," *New Yorker*, March 8, 2018. www.newyorker.com.

78. Dunckley, *Reset Your Child's Brain*, pp. 42–43.

79. Dignan, *Game Frame*, p. 33.

80. Scutti, "WHO to Recognize Gaming Disorder as Mental Health Condition in 2018."

81. Scutti, "WHO to Recognize Gaming Disorder as Mental Health Condition in 2018."

82. Scutti, "WHO to Recognize Gaming Disorder as Mental Health Condition in 2018."

83. Mackenzie Ryan, "Gaming Disorder: What Parents Should Know About Video or Online Game Addiction," *Des Moines Register,* June 21, 2018. www.desmoinesregister.com.

84. Ryan, "Gaming Disorder."

85. Ryan, "Gaming Disorder."

86. Lilly Price and Mike Snider, "Video Game Addiction Is a Mental Health Disorder, WHO Says, but Some Health Experts Don't Agree," *USA Today*, June 18, 2018. www.usatoday.com.

87. Price and Snider, "Video Game Addiction Is a Mental Health Disorder, WHO Says."

88. McGonigal, *Reality Is Broken*, p. 128.

89. McGonigal, *Reality Is Broken*, p. 129.

90. McGonigal, *Reality Is Broken*, p. 129.

91. McGonigal, *Reality Is Broken*, p. 130.

92. Dignan, *Game Frame*, p. 167.

CHAPTER 4: THE FUTURE OF YOUTH AND VIDEO GAMES

93. Beck and Wade, *Got Game: How the Gamer Generation Is Reshaping Business Forever*, p. 8.

94. McGonigal, *Reality Is Broken*, p. 14.

95. Dignan, *Game Frame*, p. 167.

96. McGonigal, *Reality Is Broken*, p. 163.

97. Jacqueline Howard, "Kids Under 9 Spend More Than 2 Hours a Day on Screens, Report Shows," *CNN*, October 19, 2017. www.cnn.com.

98. Howard, "Kids Under 9 Spend More Than 2 Hours a Day on Screens."

99. Howard, "Kids Under 9 Spend More Than 2 Hours a Day on Screens."

100. Dignan, *Game Frame*, pp. 18–19.

101. Eric Thurm, "An Alternate Reality Game That Takes Freshman Orientation to a New Level," *Wired*, March 25, 2018. www.wired.com.

102. McGonigal, *Reality Is Broken*, p. 125.

103. Robin McKie, "Virtual Reality Headsets Could Put Children's Health at Risk," *Guardian*, October 28, 2017. www.theguardian.com.

104. McKie, "Virtual Reality Headsets Could Put Children's Health at Risk."

105. McKie, "Virtual Reality Headsets Could Put Children's Health at Risk."

106. Sandee LaMotte, "The Very Real Health Dangers of Virtual Reality," *CNN*, December 13, 2017. www.cnn.com.

107. LaMotte, "The Very Real Health Dangers of Virtual Reality."

108. LaMotte, "The Very Real Health Dangers of Virtual Reality."

109. Haydn Taylor, "Hawaii Proposes Landmark Legislation Against Loot Boxes," *GamesIndustry.biz*, February 15, 2018. www.gamesindustry.biz.

110. Michael Brestovansky, "Bills Target Video Games with Rewards for a Price," *Hawaii Tribune Herald*, February 12, 2018. www.hawaiitribune-herald.com.

111. Brestovansky, "Bills Target Video Games with Rewards for a Price."

112. Max Wasserman, "Are Video-Game Loot Boxes a Form of Gambling That Targets Children? Washington Aims to Find Out," *News Tribune*, January 24, 2018. www.thenewstribune.com.

113. Wasserman, "Are Video-Game Loot Boxes a Form of Gambling That Targets Children?"

114. Singer, "Maryland Schools May Tell Children When It's Time to Log Off."

115. Singer, "Maryland Schools May Tell Children When It's Time to Log Off."

116. Beck, "With MinecraftEdu, Are Video Games the Future of Education?"

117. Devin Thorpe, "Why This Founder Thinks She Can Make a Good Educational Kid's Game," *Forbes.com*, February 1, 2017. www.forbes.com.

118. Thorpe, "Why This Founder Thinks She Can Make a Good Educational Kid's Game."

119. Rhett Allain, "Fun Ideas That Keep Kids Learning Even After School's Out," *Wired*, May 17, 2018. www.wired.com.

120. McGonigal, *Reality Is Broken*, p. 354.

FOR FURTHER RESEARCH

BOOKS

Aaron Dignan, *Game Frame: Using Games as a Strategy for Success*. New York: Free Press, 2011.

Victoria L. Dunckley, *Reset Your Child's Brain*. Novato, CA: New World Library, 2015.

P.J. Graham, *Video Game Addiction*. San Diego, CA: ReferencePoint Press, 2019.

Roland Li, *Good Luck Have Fun: The Rise of eSports*. New York: Skyhorse Publishing, 2016.

Jane McGonigal, *Reality Is Broken: Why Games Make Us Better and How They Can Change the World*. New York: Penguin, 2011.

INTERNET SOURCES

"2017 Sales, Demographic, and Usage Data: Essential Facts About the Computer and Video Game Industry," *Entertainment Software Association*, April 2017. www.theesa.com.

Anna Brown, "Younger Men Play Video Games, But So Do a Diverse Group of Other Americans," *Pew Research Center*, September 11, 2017. www.pewresearch.org.

David Lazarus, "Are Video Games Bad for Your Kids? Not So Much, Experts Now Believe," *Los Angeles Times*, November 17, 2017. www.latimes.com.

Greg Toppo, "Do Violent Video Games Make Kids Violent? Trump Thinks They Could," *USA Today*, February 20, 2018. www.usatoday.com.

"Video Game History," *History*, n.d. www.history.com.

RELATED ORGANIZATIONS AND WEBSITES

American Psychological Association

750 First St. NE
Washington, D.C. 20002-4242
www.apa.org

The American Psychological Association (APA) is a professional organization
that represents researchers, educators, and clinicians in the field of
psychology. It studies and provides comments on mental health matters,
such as video games and their effect on youth.

Entertainment Software Association

601 Massachusetts Ave. NW, Suite 300
Washington, D.C. 20001
www.theesa.com

The Entertainment Software Association (ESA) is an organization that
represents the US video game industry.

MIT Media Lab

77 Massachusetts Ave., E14/E15
Cambridge, MA 02139-4307
www.media.mit.edu

The MIT Media Lab is a part of the Massachusetts Institute of Technology.
Its researchers created Scratch, which allows youth to create their own
websites, animations, and video games.

World Health Organization

Avenue Appia 20
1202 Geneva
www.who.int

The World Health Organization (WHO) is an international health organization
which studies issues that affect public health, such as gaming disorder and
video game addiction.

INDEX

INDEX CONTINUED

ABOUT THE AUTHOR

Ashley Strehle Hartman is a journalist and writer. She's written for newspapers, government agencies, and advertising firms. When she's not writing for work, she's writing for fun. She writes an entertainment column for a local newspaper and blogs about baking. She lives in Nebraska with her husband and their dog.